BAA CHAMPIONSHIP:

↓

1947

↓

NBA CHAMPIONSHIPS:

↓

1956, 1975, 2015, 2017

↓

ALL-TIME LEADING SCORER:

↓

WILT CHAMBERLAIN (1959–65):

↓

17,783 POINTS

THE NBA:
A HISTORY
OF HOOPS
GOLDEN STATE
WARRIORS

THE NBA: A HISTORY OF HOOPS

GOLDEN STATE WARRIORS

BY JIM WHITING

CREATIVE EDUCATION CREATIVE PAPERBACKS

Published by Creative Education
and Creative Paperbacks

P.O. Box 227, Mankato, Minnesota 56002

Creative Education and Creative Paperbacks
are imprints of The Creative Company

www.thecreativecompany.us

Design and production by Blue Design
Printed in the United States of America

Photographs by AP Images (AP Photo, ASSOCIATED
PRESS), Corbis (Bettmann), Getty Images (Andrew
D. Bernstein/NBAE, Garrett Ellwood, Garrett W.
Ellwood/NBAE, Jesse D. Garrabrant/NBAE, Harry
How/Getty Images Sport, George Long/Sports
Illustrated, Ronald Martinez, John W. McDonough/
Sports Illustrated, Jason Miller/Getty Images
Sport, NBAPhotos/NBAE, Panoramic Images, Hy
Peskin/Sports Illustrated, Dick Raphael/NBAE,
Ezra Shaw/Getty Images Sport, Kent Smith/
NBAE, Justin Sullivan, Rocky Widner/NBAE),
Newscom (Christopher Chung/ZUMA Press)

Library of Congress Cataloging-in-Publication Data

Names: Whiting, Jim, 1943- author.

Title: Golden State Warriors / Jim Whiting.

Series: The NBA: A History of Hoops.

Includes bibliographical references and index.

Summary: This high-interest title summarizes the
history of the Golden State Warriors professional
basketball team, highlighting memorable events
and noteworthy players such as Stephen Curry.

Identifiers: LCCN 2016054009 / ISBN 978-1-
60818-844-4 (hardcover) / ISBN 978-1-62832-447-1
(pbk) / ISBN 978-1-56660-892-3 (eBook)

Subjects: LCSH: 1. Golden State Warriors
(Basketball team)—History—Juvenile
literature. 2. Golden State Warriors (Basketball
team)—Biography—Juvenile literature.

Classification: LCC GV885.52.G64 W45 2017 /
DDC 796.323/64097946—dc23

CCSS: RI.4.1, 2, 3, 4; RI.5.1, 2, 4; RI.6.1, 2,
3; RF.4.3, 4; RF.5.3, 4; RH. 6-8. 4, 5, 7

First Edition HC 9 8 7 6 5 4 3 2 1
First Edition PBK 9 8 7 6 5 4 3 2 1

CONTENTS

OFF TO BATTLE 9

WILT THE STILT 16

GO WEST, YOUNG MEN! 24

A TARNISHED STATE. 31

RESTORING THE SHINE 36

THE SPHAS 12

PITCHIN' PAUL 19

A DOMINANT FORCE 23

LIKE FATHER, LIKE SONS 29

HIPPIN' AND HOPPIN' TO THE HOOP 34

THE SPLASH BROTHERS 40

SELECTED BIBLIOGRAPHY 46

WEBSITES. 47

INDEX 48

LEGENDS OF THE HARDWOOD

The city of **OAKLAND** sits across the bay from San Francisco in the Golden State.

OFF TO BATTLE

Hershey, Pennsylvania, is the home of the Hershey Company. On March 2, 1962, the "Sweetest Place on Earth" also played host to the Philadelphia Warriors. The Warriors played in the

During **WILT CHAMBERLAIN'S** 100-point game, his teammates scored 69 points.

10

National Basketball Association (NBA). To attract more fans, the team played some games outside Philadelphia. That night, Warriors center Wilt Chamberlain scored 41 points by halftime! In the locker room, guard Guy Rodgers said, "Let's get the ball to Dip [Chamberlain]. Let's see how many he can get." It didn't take long to find out. Chamberlain scored 28 points in the third quarter. The New York Knicks couldn't figure out how to stop him. The crowd screamed "Give it to Wilt! Give it to Wilt!" His teammates responded. His point total kept rising. At last, Chamberlain scored a field goal with 46 seconds remaining. He had just scored 100 points! In more than 50 years since then, no one has come close to matching that total. That night defined Chamberlain as a player. "I get constant reminders from fans who equate that game and my career as one and the same," he said years later. "That's my tag, whether I like it or not."

LEGENDS OF THE HARDWOOD

THE SPHAS

Eddie Gottlieb (far right) loved playing high school basketball. He and two friends formed a team when they graduated. After the South Philadelphia Hebrew Association donated uniforms, the team became known as the Sphas. It toured the East and Midwest. People who were prejudiced against Jews didn't like the team, though. Some threw beer bottles. "There was a lady in the front row with hat pins," said team member Harry Litwack. "She used to jab you when you went by." In 1933, the Sphas joined the American Basketball League. They won 7 of the next 13 championships. After Gottlieb became the Warriors' coach and took his best players with him, the Sphas folded.

Philadelphia businessman Peter Tyrrell founded the team in 1946. It was a member of the newly formed Basketball Association of America (BAA). Tyrrell hired Eddie Gottlieb as general manager and coach. Gottlieb named the new team the Warriors. A team he founded in 1918 called the Sphas had briefly been the Warriors. He wanted to honor that team. The name may also have referred to a tribe of Delaware Indians who lived in the Philadelphia area before white settlers forced them out. The Warriors got off to a good start. Their 35–25 record placed second in the league's Eastern Division. The Warriors upended the St. Louis Bombers and New York Knicks in the first two rounds of the playoffs. They crushed the Chicago Stags four games to one to claim the BAA title. Rookie forward "Jumpin' Joe" Fulks set a league record of 37 points in just his eighth game. He also finished as the league's scoring leader with an average of 23.2 points a game. "He made one-handed shots, jump shots, right-handed [and] left-handed set shots from a distance, driving shots,

Known for his hook shot, **NEIL JOHNSTON** led the NBA in scoring for three years.

15

hooks with his right or left hand," said Gottlieb. "He was also basketball's first jump shooter."

Philadelphia advanced to the league finals again the following season. But it lost to the Baltimore Bullets. The Warriors fell to 28–32 in 1948–49. They were eliminated in the first round of the playoffs. After the season, the BAA merged with the rival National Basketball League (NBL) to form the NBA. The Warriors struggled to a 26–42 mark in their first NBA season. One of the few highlights was Fulks's 63-point game. It remained an NBA record for a decade. Another famous jump shooter, forward "Pitchin' Paul" Arizin, joined the team in 1950. The Warriors rebounded to 40–26 but were quickly eliminated from the playoffs. After going 33–33 in 1951–52 and another early playoff exit, the Warriors endured three years of losing basketball. One consolation was center Neil Johnston. He was the league leader in scoring for three straight years between 1953 and 1955.

WILT THE STILT

In the NBA's early days, some teams struggled with low attendance. But college basketball was popular. League officials thought it would help if college stars played for nearby pro teams when they

TOM V RANGERS \ DETROIT
WED RANGERS \ CHICAGO
THURS MANHATTAN \ ST PETER S
N Y U \ FORDHAM
ERI ROXING TERRELL \ ZECH

NEW YORK
23

SAN FRANCISCO
13

CHAMBERLAIN'S 23,924 career rebounds still topped the NBA charts in 2017.

graduated. Fans of those players would want to keep watching them. So the NBA modified the territorial pick rule in 1955. It allowed teams to exchange their first-round pick in the annual draft for standout local college players. The Warriors took advantage of the new rule. They drafted forward/guard Tom Gola of La Salle University. Gola had been a high scorer in college. Now he let Johnston and Arizin do much of the scoring. He focused on defense, passing, and rebounding. The formula paid off. The Warriors surged to a 45–27 mark in 1955–56. They went on to win the NBA title. They beat the Fort Wayne Pistons four games to one. Fans looked forward to more titles. But the Boston Celtics were getting hot. The Celtics defeated the Warriors in the conference finals for 1957–58. Philadelphia plunged to a 32–40 record the following season.

In the 1959 NBA Draft, the Warriors took advantage of the territorial pick rule again. Wilt Chamberlain had grown up in Philadelphia. He was called "Wilt the Stilt" because he stood 7-foot-1. He attended the University of Kansas. In his first college game, he scored 52 points and hauled down 31 rebounds. He left Kansas after his junior year. He couldn't join the NBA right away. He had to wait until his class graduated. He played a year with the Harlem Globetrotters. Then the Warriors claimed him. He scored 43 points and grabbed 28 rebounds in his first game. The team went from 32 wins the previous season to 49. Chamberlain made

LEGENDS OF THE HARDWOOD

PITCHIN' PAUL

PAUL ARIZIN, SMALL FORWARD, 6-FOOT-4, 1950–62

Paul Arizin grew up playing pickup basketball. The gym floors were so slick that Arizin kept slipping. Then he discovered something: "I found that by leaving my feet when I shot I could avoid slipping," he said. "The more I did it, the better I became, and before you knew it, practically all my shots were jump shots." His accuracy gave him the nickname "Pitchin' Paul." As a junior at Villanova University, Arizin was named College Player of the Year. He was just as successful as a pro. He went on to average 20 or more points a game for nine years. The 10-time All-Star joined the NBA Hall of Fame in 1978.

The Warriors defeated the Pistons four games to one for their first NBA title.

a clean sweep of the major awards. He was named Rookie of the Year, Most Valuable Player (MVP), and All-Star Game MVP. He also began what is perhaps the most famous individual rivalry in NBA history, with fellow center Bill Russell of the Celtics.

Russell and the Celtics defeated Chamberlain and the Warriors in the 1960 Eastern Division finals, four games to two. Chamberlain averaged 30 points a game. Russell averaged 20. That became a common pattern. Chamberlain usually outscored Russell. But the Celtics had better teamwork. There would be no rematch the following season. Syracuse swept the Warriors 3–0 in the division semifinals. The Celtics and Warriors met again in the division finals in 1962. Once again, Chamberlain held the scoring advantage over Russell. Once again, the Celtics won the series. They took the decisive

Coach **FRANK McGUIRE** led the Warriors to 49 wins during the 1961–62 season.

seventh game 109–107. One factor was a tactic the Celtics used against Chamberlain. "We went for his weakness," said Celtics forward Tom Heinsohn. "We tried to send him to the foul line, and in doing that he took the most brutal pounding of any player ever. I hear people today talk about hard fouls. Half the fouls against him were hard fouls."

LEGENDS OF THE HARDWOOD

A DOMINANT FORCE

WILT CHAMBERLAIN, CENTER, 7-FOOT-1, 1959–65

Someone once asked Hall-of-Famer Oscar Robertson if Wilt Chamberlain was the greatest NBA player. "The books don't lie," Robertson said. Chamberlain's name is all over the NBA record books. The only player to score 4,000 points in a season. The league's all-time leading rebounder. Perhaps his most remarkable stat was that he never fouled out of a game. "My friends would say, 'Hey man, you should throw [Bill] Russell in the basket, too,'" he said. "They said I was too nice." But being mean wasn't Chamberlain. Not even when he appeared in the 1984 movie *Conan the Destroyer*. He played the character Bombaata, who is ordered to kill Conan. But of course he doesn't.

24

GO WEST, YOUNG MEN!

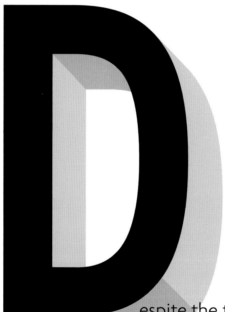

Despite the team's success and Chamberlain's obvious star power, the Warriors didn't sell enough tickets. San Francisco Bay area radio and TV producer Franklin Mieuli bought the team in 1962.

Versatile big man **NATE THURMOND** could block shots, grab rebounds, and score points.

In the 1975 Finals, **RICK BARRY** scored 29.5 points per game and earned Finals MVP honors.

"THAT WAS A POWERFUL, PHYSICAL TEAM," SAID BOSTON COACH ARNOLD "RED" AUERBACH. "CHAMBERLAIN AND THURMOND WERE TWO OF THE BEST CENTERS IN THE GAME."

He moved it to San Francisco and changed the name to the San Francisco Warriors. The Warriors' first season on the West Coast went south. The team struggled to a 31–49 mark. San Francisco drafted 6-foot-11 power forward/center Nate Thurmond to help Chamberlain. The Warriors improved to 48–32. They won the Western Division finals and once again faced Boston. This time, the NBA title was on the line. "That was a powerful, physical team," said Boston coach Arnold "Red" Auerbach. "Chamberlain and Thurmond were two of the best centers in the game." But Boston won the series four games to one. The Warriors got off to a slow start in 1964–65. They traded Chamberlain. He went back home to Philadelphia to join the 76ers. The team had just moved there from Syracuse. The trade paved the way for Thurmond to emerge from Chamberlain's shadow and become a dominating force.

Two years later, the Warriors met the 76ers in the NBA Finals. Chamberlain was the centerpiece of a team that swept to an NBA-record 68 wins. San Francisco had a new star, forward Rick Barry. He had been selected as Rookie of the Year the previous season. Nicknamed the "Golden Gunner" for his blond hair, Barry averaged 40 points a game in the series. But the Warriors were no match for the 76ers. They lost the series four games to two. Barry left the following season in a contract dispute. The Warriors still advanced to the Western Division finals. However, the Los Angeles Lakers swept them in four games.

Coach **AL ATTLES** trained his team to have the speed and stamina to outlast opponents.

After several so-so seasons, in 1971, the Warriors settled permanently into the Oakland Coliseum Arena. They changed their name to Golden State Warriors. "Golden State" is California's official nickname. Mieuli hoped the name change would broaden his team's appeal. The Warriors improved. They advanced to the conference finals in 1973. Once again, they had to face Chamberlain. He had been traded to the Lakers. The Lakers easily won the series, four games to one.

Two years later, the Warriors swept through the conference playoffs. Center Clifford Ray anchored the defense. Rookie of the Year forward Jamaal Wilkes provided scoring punch. So did Barry, who had rejoined the team. The Warriors faced the heavily favored Washington Bullets in the NBA Finals. In a stunning upset, Golden State swept the series, 4–0. Two wins were by a single point. "We cared about winning and did whatever we could to win," said Barry. "It was an atmosphere you'd like to see more professional teams have. I defy anyone to find anything like it."

LEGENDS OF THE HARDWOOD

LIKE FATHER, LIKE SONS

Rick Barry's first four sons all played professional hoops. The oldest, Richard "Scooter" Barry, had a 17-year career. He played in two American minor leagues, several European leagues, and even a season in Australia. In Jon Barry's 14-year NBA career, he averaged 5.7 points per game. Brent Barry also played 14 years in the NBA, with 6 teams. In 2005, he and his dad became just the second father-son duo to win an NBA championship as players. Drew Barry's seven-year career included several seasons in Europe and brief stints with three NBA teams. Barry's fifth son, Canyon, graduated from college in 2017. His path was yet to be determined.

High-scoring guard **JEFF MULLINS** was a three-time All-Star with the Warriors.

A TARNISHED STATE

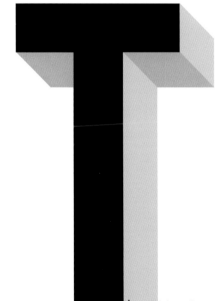

The Warriors went 59–23 the following season. It was the best record in team history. But they lost the Western Conference championship to Phoenix, four games to three. They couldn't get

Guard **TIM HARDAWAY'S** fast moves made it hard for opponents to stop him.

past the conference semifinals in 1976–77. That was the last time the Warriors would see the playoffs for nine seasons. The low point came in 1984–85: Golden State won just 22 games.

One trade seemed to symbolize the team's lack of accomplishment. Before the 1980 NBA Draft, the Warriors traded rising star center Robert Parish and their third overall pick to Boston. In return, the Celtics gave Golden State the top overall pick and the 13th pick. The Warriors took Purdue center Joe Barry Carroll with the top pick. They added Mississippi forward/center Rickey Brown with the 13th. Carroll appeared to be a productive addition to the team. In 6 seasons, he averaged more than 20 points a game. Nevertheless, many people consider him one of the biggest busts in NBA Draft history. One reason was that he hardly ever seemed to put out much effort. He was nicknamed "Joe Barely Cares." Brown was a flop. He was traded after two seasons. On the other hand, Boston drafted forward Kevin McHale. He and Parish formed part of a dominant front line for the Celtics for more than a decade. They had a combined 16 All-Star Game selections. Making that draft even worse, the Warriors traded away center Jeff Ruland to Washington. Ruland made the All-Rookie first team and was a two-time All-Star.

Golden State hired George Karl as coach in 1986–87. The team compiled a 42–40 record. It defeated the Utah Jazz in the first round of

34

HIPPIN' AND HOPPIN' TO THE HOOP

In 1983, the three-man hip-hop group Run–D.M.C. released its first single. The group had hits such as "Walk This Way" and "You Be Illin.'" They were still popular by 1989. That year, the Warriors formed their own super-trio. Guard Tim Hardaway was the lightning-quick ball handler. Guard Mitch Richmond excelled at slashing to the basket. Forward Chris Mullin was a deadly outside sharpshooter. In 1990–91, "Run TMC" combined for an average of 72.5 points per game. That made them the highest-scoring trio in NBA history. "The magical union is still being celebrated," wrote Scott Howard-Cooper of nba.com in 2011. "That's not a bad legacy: two seasons enough to carry decades."

the playoffs. The Warriors faced the Lakers in the second round. Guard Eric "Sleepy" Floyd established two NBA playoff records in one of the games. He scored 29 points in a quarter, 39 in a half. The Warriors won, 129–121. But the Lakers scooped up the rest of the semifinals series and went on to capture the NBA title. Karl left the following year. He was angry because the team traded away most of its top scorers.

Karl's replacement, Don Nelson, put together an exciting, high-scoring, young team. The Warriors made the playoffs fairly consistently. But they couldn't ever make it past the Western Conference semifinals. When the team dropped to 26–56 in 1994–95, Nelson was fired.

36

RESTORING THE SHINE

 hat was the start of one of the worst stretches of basketball in NBA history. The team failed to qualify for the playoffs for 12 years in a row. Only the Los Angeles Clippers had a longer streak. Three times

37

Fans chanted "We Believe" when the Warriors returned to the playoffs in 2006–07 after a 12-year slump.

MONTA ELLIS attacked the rim for nearly 20 points per game over 7 seasons.

GOLDEN STATE MADE ONE OF ITS BEST DRAFT DECISIONS IN 2009. IT CHOSE GUARD STEPHEN CURRY WITH THE SEVENTH OVERALL PICK.

the Warriors didn't win even 20 games. Twice they won just 21. One of the few highlights of this dark era came in 2002–03. Guard Gilbert Arenas was named the NBA's Most Improved Player. It was just his second season with Golden State. But a contract technicality let him leave. He went on to become a three-time All-Star. Finally, in 2006–07, the Warriors finished 42–40 and beat the Dallas Mavericks in the first round of the playoffs. But the Jazz played bad music in the second round. They defeated Golden State four games to one. That set off another losing streak. This one lasted five seasons.

Help was on the way. Golden State made one of its best draft decisions in 2009. It chose guard Stephen Curry with the seventh overall pick. Even with Curry, the Warriors kept losing. But they kept making good draft decisions. They drafted guard Klay Thompson in 2011. They took forwards Harrison Barnes and Draymond Green the following year. Golden State finally had a winning record in 2012–13. "It's inspiring to think of what we were able to accomplish this year and the foundation that has been laid," said coach Mark Jackson.

40

THE SPLASH BROTHERS

STEPHEN CURRY, POINT GUARD, 6-FOOT-3, 2009–PRESENT
KLAY THOMPSON, SHOOTING GUARD, 6-FOOT-7, 2011–PRESENT

Stephen Curry and Klay Thompson may not be related, but as the "Splash Brothers" they know how to "splash" the net, especially on three-pointers. In 2014–15, Curry and Thompson set an NBA record for their 525 combined three-point shots. They broke their own record the following year, with 603. "The way the two of them shoot the ball and ... how quick their release is and how deep their range is, it's unique," Miami Heat coach Erik Spoelstra said. The two teammates have other things in common: Their dads, Dell Curry and Mychal Thompson, enjoyed long pro basketball careers. Their mothers, Sonya Curry and Julie Thompson, played college volleyball.

LEGENDS OF THE HARDWOOD

STEPHEN CURRY led the league in 3-point shots five years in a row.

till, hardly anyone was prepared for what happened in 2014–15. The Warriors surged to a 67–15 record. Curry was named the league's MVP. The Warriors lost just three games in the first three rounds of the playoffs. They met superstar LeBron James and the Cleveland Cavaliers in the Finals. The Cavs won two of the first three contests. Then the Warriors surged back to win three in a row and take the championship. According to *New York Times* basketball writer John Branch, it was "as if the Warriors had

ANDREW BOGUT and DRAYMOND GREEN combined for 16.5 rebounds per game in 2015–16.

caught the rest of the NBA off-guard with their small lineups and free-spirited style."

Golden State kept its momentum in 2015–16. On November 24, the Warriors swamped the Lakers 111–77. It was their 16th win in a row. That broke the NBA record for consecutive wins to start the season. When the Warriors reached 21 wins, they set a record for the best start in any major pro sports league. That became the springboard for a 73–9 season. It broke the NBA record of 72 wins, set by Chicago in 1995–96. "Never

One of the best shooters in the NBA, **CURRY** became the face of the Warriors.

The Warriors added scoring punch with star forward **KEVIN DURANT** in 2016–17.

> IT WAS "AS IF THE WARRIORS HAD CAUGHT THE REST OF THE NBA OFF-GUARD WITH THEIR SMALL LINEUPS AND FREE-SPIRITED STYLE."

in a million years would [I] have guessed that that record would ever be broken," said Warriors coach Steve Kerr. He played for that Bulls team! Curry set yet another NBA mark with 402 three-pointers. He became the first unanimous selection as MVP. But Golden State couldn't get past the Cleveland Cavaliers in the Finals. The Warriors became the first team to hold a 3–1 edge in the Finals and lose the series. The Cavs' LeBron James had one of the greatest-ever Finals performances, while Curry played well below his regular-season form. "It wasn't easy what we accomplished [in the regular season]," Curry said, "and it's not an easy pill to swallow what we didn't accomplish [in the Finals]." The loss connected Golden State with the 2001 Seattle Mariners and 2007–08 New England Patriots. The three teams set all-time records for regular-season wins but didn't win their respective league championships.

The Warriors signed superstar Kevin Durant during the off-season. Golden State roared through the first 3 rounds of the playoffs, sweeping all 12 games. No team had ever done that before. Durant proved his worth in the Finals against Cleveland. He scored more than 30 points in each of the 5 games as the Warriors won their second title in 3 years.

And they might have been just getting warmed up. "I see nothing preventing them from going to 8 to 10 straight Finals," said former coach and TV analyst Jeff Van Gundy. That's good news for the team's fans. It's bad news for the rest of the NBA.

SELECTED BIBLIOGRAPHY

Ballard, Chris. *The Art of a Beautiful Game: The Thinking Fan's Tour of the NBA*. New York: Simon & Schuster, 2010.

Hareas, John. *Ultimate Basketball: More Than 100 Years of the Sport's Evolution*. New York: DK, 2004.

Hubbard, Jan, ed. *The Official NBA Basketball Encyclopedia*. 3rd edition. New York: Doubleday, 2000.

NBA.com. "Golden State Warriors." http://www.nba .com/warriors/.

Simmons, Bill. *The Book of Basketball: The NBA According to the Sports Guy*. New York: Ballantine, 2009.

Sports Illustrated. *Sports Illustrated Basketball's Greatest*. New York: Sports Illustrated, 2014.

WEBSITES

DUCKSTERS BASKETBALL: NBA
http://www.ducksters.com/sports/national_basketball_association.php

Learn more about NBA history, rules, positions, strategy, drills, and other topics.

JR. NBA
http://jr.nba.com/

This kids site has games, videos, game results, team and player information, statistics, and more.

Note: Every effort has been made to ensure that any websites listed above were active at the time of publication. However, because of the nature of the Internet, it is impossible to guarantee that these sites will remain active indefinitely or that their contents will not be altered.

INDEX

All-Star Game 21, 32

Arenas, Gilbert 39

Arizin, "Pitchin' Paul" 15, 18, 19

BAA seasons 13, 15

    championships 13

Barnes, Harrison 39

Barry, Rick 27, 28, 29

Brown, Rickey 32

Carroll, Joe Barry 32

Chamberlain, Wilt 10, 18, 21, 22, 23, 24, 27, 28

Curry, Stephen 39, 40, 41, 45

Durant, Kevin 45

Floyd, Eric "Sleepy" 35

Fulks, "Jumpin' Joe" 13, 15

Gola, Tom 18

Gottlieb, Eddie 12, 13, 15

Green, Draymond 39

Hardaway, Tim 34

Jackson, Mark 39

Johnston, Neil 15, 18

Karl, George 32, 35

Kerr, Steve 45

Mieuli, Frank 24, 28

Mullin, Chris 34

MVP award 21, 41, 45

NBA championships 18, 28, 29, 41, 45

NBA Draft 18, 27, 32, 39

NBA Finals 27, 28, 41, 45

NBA records 10, 23, 40, 42, 45

Nelson, Don 35

Oakland Coliseum Arena 28

Parish, Robert 32

Philadelphia seasons 9–10, 13, 15, 18, 27, 28

    relocation to Oakland 28

    relocation to San Francisco 27

playoffs 13, 15, 18, 21–22, 27, 28, 31–32, 35, 39, 41, 45

Ray, Clifford 28

Richmond, Mitch 34

Rodgers, Guy 10

Rookie of the Year award 21, 27, 28

Ruland, Jeff 32

team name 13, 27, 28

Thompson, Klay 39, 40

Thurmond, Nate 27

Tyrrell, Peter 13

Wilkes, Jamaal 28

48